A GUIDE TO
THE NEW TRANSLATION

of

THE MASS

EDWARD SRI

West Chester, Pennsylvania

Nihil obstat: Mr. William Beckman
                       Censor Deputatus

Imprimatur: +Most Reverend Charles J. Chaput, O.F.M. Cap.
                       Archbishop of Denver
                       January 21, 2011

Published by Ascension Press
Post Office Box 1990
West Chester, PA 19380
Orders: 1-800-376-0520
www.AscensionPress.com
www.BibleStudyforCatholics.com

Cover design: Devin Schadt

Printed in the United States of America
ISBN 978-1-935940-04-3

Contents

Introduction

"*D*o *this in memory of me.*" These remarkable words were spoken by Jesus nearly 2,000 years ago when he instituted the Eucharist at the Last Supper. The Church fulfills this command of the Lord whenever we celebrate the Mass. In doing so, we participate in the supreme mystery of our faith, the memorial of Christ's passion, death, and resurrection.

The way in which the Mass is celebrated has undergone various changes throughout the centuries, but the heart of the liturgy has remained the same. It continues to be a celebration of the banquet of the Lord, in which Catholics come to hear the word of God in the Scriptures and receive the body and blood of Christ in the Eucharist. As we prepare to welcome the revised English translation of the Mass, we can be assured that the Eucharist we celebrate will stand in continuity with that first Eucharist instituted by Christ—and that the new translation is intended to help enhance our worship of God and deepen our participation in the sacred mysteries of the liturgy.

This booklet seeks to explain why the new translation of the Mass is being issued and how it will affect the various parts of the Mass. It will also consider the meaning of some of the more noticeable changes and how they will assist our worship. It is my prayer that this booklet will help you develop not only a greater awareness of the upcoming changes in the translation of the Mass, but also a deeper appreciation for the Liturgy itself and a deeper love for Jesus in the Eucharist.

Questions and Answers

1. Is the Mass changing?

The essence of the Mass is not changing, but the way it is celebrated will be noticeably different. While the structure and order of the Mass will remain the same, many of the prayers and responses of the liturgy have been newly translated into English from the original Latin text. In addition, new observances for recently canonized saints, additional prefaces for the Eucharistic prayers, additional Masses for various needs and intentions, and updated instructions for the overall celebration of the Mass will be added. The most significant change people will notice, however, is the new translation of the actual words of the Mass.

2. So the Mass we celebrate in English is a translation from the Latin?

Yes. In the Roman rite of the Church, the Mass was celebrated in Latin for centuries. After the Second Vatican Council in the 1960s, the prayers of the liturgy were translated into the vernacular (or "common") language of a given country to encourage more active participation by the people. The official Latin text of the Mass is contained in a book known as the *Roman Missal* or *Missale Romanum* (from the Latin word *missalis*, meaning "pertaining to the Mass"). This is the foundational text from which bishops around the world commission translations of the Mass into local languages.

3. How significant will the changes in the Mass parts be?

The new translation will bring about the most significant change in the way most English-speaking Catholics participate in the Mass since the years following the Second Vatican Council (1962–1965), when the liturgical texts were translated into English and officially used in worship for the first time. When the new translation is implemented, we will see how almost all of the prayers have been affected by it. The basic structure of the prayers will for the most part remain the same, but the change in wording at many points throughout the liturgy will be quite noticeable. For a time, most Catholics will no longer be able to walk into church on Sunday and automatically recite the *Gloria*, the Creed, and other Mass parts by memory. They will need a guide to help them become accustomed to the new translation of these prayers.

4. Why do we need a *new* translation?

When the Second Vatican Council allowed for "a more extended use of the mother tongue within the Mass" (*Sacrosanctum Concilium*, no. 53), various groups worked quickly to develop an official English translation to be used for the first time in worship, and a full English missal was published in 1973. The approach to translation used at that time (known as "dynamic equivalence") aimed at communicating the general meaning of the Latin text of the Mass, rather than providing a literal, or word-for-word, translation.

After forty years of celebrating Mass in English, the Church has come to see certain areas where the English text could be improved. Some have noted that, when the Latin text was paraphrased, a number of rich spiritual metaphors and images were lost. Important theological concepts were not always clear, and several biblical allusions did not shine out as noticeably as they could.

In 2001, the Vatican called for a more precise translation that gives Catholics a better sense of the richness of the Latin text—a translation that would be "without omissions or additions in terms of their content, without paraphrases or glosses" (*Liturgiam Authenticam*, no. 20). Following this approach, the new translation of the Mass preserves more fully the theological tradition captured throughout the centuries in the liturgy. It also more clearly communicates the many biblical allusions and vital theological concepts that are expressed in the Latin original.

5. **Who is responsible for making the English translation of the Mass?**

The translation process actually entails the work of several groups. Following the issuance of Vatican II's Constitution on the Sacred Liturgy (*Sacrosanctum Concilium*) in 1963, the bishops' conferences in several English-speaking countries commissioned a Vatican-approved organization known as the International Commission on English in the Liturgy (ICEL) to prepare preliminary translations of the Mass. These translations are then reviewed, modified, and approved by each country's conference of bishops. They are then sent to Rome for final approval by the Congregation for Divine Worship and the Discipline of the Sacraments, the Vatican office that oversees all matters concerning the celebration of the liturgy.

The Congregation is assisted by a subcommittee of bishops and consultants from the English-speaking world known as *Vox Clara* ("Clear Voice").

6. **What are some examples of the changes made to the prayers of the Mass?**

A change everyone will notice at the very beginning of Mass is the people's response to the priest's greeting, "The Lord be with you." In place of the words "And also with you," the congregation will reply, "And with your spirit"—wording that better reflects the biblical language of St. Paul in his letters (see Galatians 6:18; Philippians 4:23; 2 Timothy 4:22) and recognizes the unique work of the Holy Spirit through the ordained priest to celebrate the Eucharist.

People will also notice a change in the opening word of the Nicene Creed. Instead of saying "*We* believe in one God...," the congregation will begin "*I* believe in one God...," a more personal expression of faith—as well as a more literal translation of the Latin text of the Creed.

A commentary on the major changes to the English text of the Mass begins on page 10. In addition, a tear-out chart containing all of the new people's parts of the Mass can be found at the end of this booklet.

7. **Will these changes affect the music for the parts of the Mass?**

Yes, to some degree. Liturgical music publishers have been developing new musical settings for the newly translated prayer responses such as the *Gloria*, the Lamb of God, and other Mass parts. Many dioceses and parishes will introduce people to these new settings to prepare them for use when the new translation goes into effect. New chants also are being incorporated into the publication of the revised *Missal*.

8.   When will we start using the new translation?

The new translation will be officially promulgated for use in the liturgy on November 27, 2011, which is the first Sunday of Advent and the beginning of the Church's new liturgical year.

9.   Can I review the new translation of the Mass now?

The new translation of the Mass is posted online at the United States Conference of Catholic Bishops (USCCB) website, www.usccb.org/romanmissal. It has been made available for catechetical purposes. To avoid confusion between the current and revised versions of the Mass, however, the new translation is not permitted to be used in the liturgy until it is officially promulgated on November 27, 2011.

10.   What are some of the benefits of the new translation?

First, as previously noted, the older translation of the Mass parts does not fully convey many of the rich biblical images and allusions in the Latin original; the new translation seeks to bring these out more clearly.

Moreover, various bishops, theologians, and commentators have noted how the new translation preserves traditional theological terms such as Jesus being "consubstantial with the Father" and made "incarnate" of the Blessed Virgin Mary—terms that are important to pass down in our worship. (The significance of these and other terms is considered beginning on page 10.)

In addition, the revised translation as a whole uses a more "heightened" style of English that is less conversational and nobler in tone. This style more closely parallels the Latin text and helps us express an even greater reverence and humility in praying to God in the Mass.

All these changes are valuable. The way we worship tells us a lot about what we believe and how we view our relationship with God. As a traditional Latin expression goes, *lex orandi, lex credendi*—"the law of prayer is the law of belief." In other words, the way we pray shapes our beliefs. And what we believe affects how we live our relationship with God.

For example, when we use more informal language while praying, we might tend to relate to God in a more casual manner. But when the Mass uses more heightened language that emphasizes God's goodness, power, and glory, we may be more disposed to recognize that we are encountering the presence of the all-holy God in the sacred liturgy and to approach him with greater humility, reverence, and gratitude. Indeed, the words we use in worship express how we view ourselves in relationship to God. Thus, it was important for the Church to weigh carefully the translation of the Mass parts in this way.

Finally, a positive side effect of the new translation is that it provides the Church in the English-speaking world with a unique moment to catechize about one of the foundational aspects of our faith, but one that is often not understood well by Catholics—the Mass.

With the significant changes in the Mass parts, we will need to learn new responses and new musical settings, as well as become accustomed to hearing the priest use liturgical phrases that are different from what we have heard for nearly forty years. The upcoming period of transition can be an opportunity not merely to train us how to say new responses, but to catechize on the *meaning* of the liturgy—to help us understand the Eucharist as the sacrificial memorial of Christ's death on the cross, the real presence of Jesus in the Eucharist, and the intimate union we have with Our Lord in holy communion. It also is an opportunity to help us understand the significance of the prayers and rituals in the liturgy. The more we grasp the meaning of what we say and do in the Mass, the more we will be able to give ourselves to God in the liturgy and encounter him in these sacred mysteries.

11. How is the Church preparing for the new translation?

As we have seen, the upcoming changes to the Mass represent the most significant liturgical development in the English-speaking world since Vatican II. Educating Catholics on the changes is vitally important to the liturgical life of the Church and our personal devotional lives. This is why it is crucial for dioceses and parishes to prepare the people for these changes. The majority of dioceses have already begun training priests, religious, deacons, catechists, and other lay ministers in the details of the new translation. These and other diocesan and parish leaders will provide the laity with catechesis and resources concerning the new Mass texts.

12. What can I do personally to prepare for the new translation?

First, become educated on the actual changes in the Mass texts, especially to the people's parts (which are listed on the chart at the end of this booklet). In addition, take advantage of any workshops on the new translation offered in your parish or diocese, and seek out articles and books on the topic. The more you learn about the new Mass parts and why these changes were made, the better you will be prepared to understand and appreciate the new translation. This will help you enter more deeply into the celebration of the Mass.

Developing a deeper spiritual participation in the liturgy right now will help you benefit from the improvements we will find in the new translation. Participating in Mass every Sunday and holy day is most fundamental. Arriving a few minutes before the start of Mass to pray can help you prepare to encounter Our Lord in the Eucharist. Listening attentively to the Scripture readings and homily, receiving Jesus in holy communion reverently, and taking time for prayer and thanksgiving after communion (and even for a few moments after Mass) foster devotion to Jesus in the liturgy. These and other spiritual practices will be beneficial when the new translation is implemented and can help you appreciate and enter into the new prayers even more.

Teaching your children ahead of time about the new Mass parts will be important to help them through the transition period. This also is a wonderful opportunity for them to learn more about the Mass itself and about the meaning of what we say and do in the liturgy.

The Meaning Behind Some of the Changes

1. The Greeting (*"The Lord be with you ..."*)

One of the most noticeable changes in the Mass parts is the people's response to the priest's greeting, "The Lord be with you." In the new translation, we will reply, "And with your spirit." This more adequately reflects the Latin text of the Mass and the biblical language of St. Paul (see Galatians 6:18; Philippians 4:23; 2 Timothy 4:22).

It also more fully expresses an important theological point. When we said, "And also with you" in the older translation, one might get the impression that our response was merely intended to express an exchange of personal greetings or reciprocal good will: "May the Lord be with you, too, Father."

But there is much more to this response. When a man is ordained a priest, the Holy Spirit comes upon him in a unique way, enabling him to perform the sacred rites of the Mass and consecrate the Eucharist. By responding, "And with your spirit," we acknowledge the Spirit's activity through the priest during the sacred liturgy. It is Jesus Christ who is the head of the community gathered for Mass and it is his Spirit who is the primary actor in the liturgy, regardless who the particular priest celebrating Mass may be.

2. The *Confiteor* ("*I confess to almighty God...*")

In the prayer known as the *Confiteor* (which begins, "I confess to almighty God..."), the new translation better reflects the Latin text of the Mass and helps us cultivate a more humble, sorrowful attitude toward God as we confess our sins. Instead of simply saying that I have sinned "through my own fault," as we have in the old translation, we will now repeat it three times while striking our breasts in a sign of repentance, saying: "*Through my fault, through my fault, through my most grievous fault.*"

This repetition more fully expresses our sorrow over sin. When we are at fault over something small, we might simply say to the person whom we have wronged, "I'm sorry." But if it is a more serious matter and we *deeply* feel sorrow over our actions, we sometimes apologize several times and in varying ways: "I'm so sorry...I really regret doing that...Please forgive me." This prayer in the liturgy helps us recognize that sinning against God is no light matter. We must take responsibility for whatever wrong we have done and whatever good we failed to do. At Mass, one does not simply offer an apology to God. The revised translation of this prayer helps the Christian express even more heartfelt contrition and humbly admit that one has sinned "through my fault, through my fault, through my most grievous fault."

3. The *Gloria* ("*Glory to God in the Highest ...*")

In the new translation, Jesus is addressed as the "Only Begotten Son." This more closely follows the theological language used in the early Church to highlight how Jesus is uniquely God's Son, sharing in the same divine nature as the Father. This also reflects the biblical language in John's gospel, which uses similar wording to describe Jesus' singular relationship with the Father. While all believers are called to a special relationship with God as his sons and daughters through grace (see John 1:12; 1 John 3:1), Jesus alone is the eternal, divine Son by nature. He is the "only begotten Son" of the Father (see John 1:14, 18; 3:16, 18).

4.   The Creed *("I believe in one God ...")*

Several changes have been made to the translation of the Nicene Creed used in the Mass. Here are some of the major revisions:

"We believe" is now "I believe"

We have begun the Nicene Creed with the words "*We* believe in one God..." The new translation, however—"*I* believe in one God"—unites us with the rest of the Catholic world in using the singular. After Vatican II, English was the only Western language that translated the opening Latin word of the Creed (*Credo*, "I believe") with the plural "*We* believe." The singular "I," however, makes the Creed more personal and challenges each individual to interiorize the faith. As the *Catechism of the Catholic Church* explains, "I believe" expresses "the faith of the Church professed personally by each believer" (no. 167).

This is what we do when we renew our baptismal promises during the Easter season or when we attend a baptism. The priest asks if we believe in the various statements of faith in the Creed: "Do you believe in God the Father Almighty...?" "Do you believe in Jesus Christ...?" "Do you believe in the Holy Spirit...?" Each individual answers for himself or herself, saying, "I do." It is fitting that we will regularly make a similar personal act of faith by using the singular "I believe" whenever the Creed is recited in the Mass.

"One in being with the Father" is now "Consubstantial with the Father"

While this change involves what some may see as arcane or technical theological language, it is important to be as precise as possible when speaking about the nature of God. The revised translation of the Creed aims at helping us more precisely profess a concept about the nature of the Son and his relationship with God the Father. The previous wording referred to Jesus as "one in being with the Father." We will now speak of Jesus being "consubstantial with the Father."

So what's the difference? Simply put, the new wording more closely reflects the theological language of the bishops at the Council of Nicea (A.D. 325) who wanted to safeguard that Jesus was acknowledged as the eternal Son of God, equal to the Father. The council condemned the false teaching of a man named Arius who held that there was a time when the Son did not exist. According to Arius, God created the Son and then adopted him. He said the Son of God "came to be from things that were not" and the Son was "from another substance" than that of the Father (*Catechism*, no. 465).

In opposition to this, the Council of Nicea taught that the Son is "God from God, light from light, true God from true God" and "of the same substance" (*homoousios* in Greek) as the Father. The Son was not created by the Father, but rather is a distinct divine Person who has existed from all eternity, sharing the same divine nature with the Father and the Holy Spirit.

When *homoousios* was translated from Greek into Latin, it was rendered *consubstantialem*, which has traditionally been translated as "consubstantial" in English. The new translation of the Mass returns to this traditional rendering. Although the term "consubstantial" might not roll easily off the tongue, its use preserves the precise theological tradition of the Council of Nicea and invites us to reflect more on the divine nature of Christ and the mystery of the Trinity.

"Was born of the Virgin Mary" is now "Was incarnate of the Virgin Mary"

Another important theological term is now preserved in the new translation of the Creed's statement about Jesus' unique conception. The older translation referred to the Son in this way: "By the power of the Holy Spirit he was born of the virgin Mary, and became man." The new translation says that Jesus "by the Holy Spirit was incarnate of the Virgin Mary, and became man."

This phraseology more accurately reflects the Latin text of the Mass, which includes the word *incarnatus* ("incarnate"). This theological term refers to "the fact that the Son of God assumed a human nature in order to accomplish our salvation in it" (*Catechism*, no. 461). In the words of John's gospel, "The Word became flesh" (John 1:14). Accordingly, we now say that the Son "by the Holy Spirit was incarnate of the Virgin Mary, and became man." Not only is this a more precise translation, it also captures more of the theological point expressed in the Creed. The Son of God was not just born of the Virgin Mary; he actually took on human flesh!

5. The *Sanctus* ("Holy, Holy, Holy Lord God of Hosts...")

The opening line of the *Sanctus* is taken not from a hymn book, but from the angels' worship of God in heaven. In the Old Testament, the prophet Isaiah was given a vision of the angels praising God, crying out, "Holy, holy, holy is the LORD of hosts" (see Isaiah 6:3). The word "hosts" here refers to the heavenly army of angels. When we recite "Holy, Holy, Holy Lord" in the

Mass, therefore, we are joining the angels in heaven, echoing their very words of worship.

The previous translation of this prayer referred to the Lord as "God of power and might." In the new translation, we address him as "Lord God of hosts." This more clearly echoes the biblical language of the angels in Isaiah and underscores the infinite breadth of God's power. All things in heaven and on earth are under his dominion—including the angels, who adore him unceasingly. Indeed, he is "the Lord God of hosts."

6. The Words of Institution

Some changes have been made to the translation of the Words of Institution from the Last Supper, including the following:

"This is the cup of my Blood" is now "This is the chalice of my Blood"

While the previous translation of the Words of Institution referred to the "cup" of Christ's blood, the new translation renders it "chalice." This is a more accurate and more formal rendering of the Latin text of the Mass and one that underscores the liturgical nature of this vessel. This is no ordinary cup, but the Eucharistic cup (see Luke 22:20; 1 Corinthians 11:25ff.) that the Lord consecrated at the Last Supper. This most sacred of vessels has traditionally been called a "chalice," and this is the term used in the new translation.

"For all" is now "For many"

The previous translation of the Mass referred to Jesus' blood having redemptive value "for all." But the new translation replaces the words "for all" with "for many." This revision remains closer to Jesus' actual words of institution in the gospels (see Matthew 26:28). It is also more harmonious with the Latin text of the Mass—and with wording that has been used in the liturgy for centuries. The new rendering also has implications for understanding how Christ's saving work is applied to our lives. Some have raised concerns that the words "for many" limit the universal scope of Jesus' saving mission. They hold that the new wording gives the impression that Jesus did not die on the cross for everyone—that he offered his blood on Calvary not "for all" but just for a select group of people, "for many." This is a misunderstanding of the text.

The new translation points to the reality that while Jesus died for all, not everyone chooses to accept this gift. Each individual must choose to welcome the gift of salvation in Christ and live according to that grace, so that they may be among "the many" who are described in this text.

Moreover, a number of Scripture scholars have observed that Jesus' language at the Last Supper about his blood being poured out "for many" recalls "the many" that are three times mentioned in Isaiah 53:11-12.* In this prophecy, Isaiah foretold that God one day would send his servant who would make himself "an offering for sin," bearing the sin of "many" and making "many" righteous (Isaiah 53:10-12). Jesus, by speaking at the Last Supper about his own blood being poured out "for many," was associating himself with this "suffering servant" figure prophesied by Isaiah. Jesus is the one who offers his life for the "many." This should not be understood in opposition to the fact that Jesus died "for all" (1 Timothy 2:6). The other prophecies in Isaiah about the Servant of the Lord make clear that he has a universal mission, one that announces salvation to *all* humanity (see, for example, Isaiah 42:1-10, 49:6, 52:10). In this context, the expression "the many" can be seen

---

* The Greek Septuagint translation of the Old Testament uses the word *polloi* ("many") three times in these verses.

as contrasting the *one* person who dies—the Lord's Servant (Jesus)—with *the many* who benefit from his atoning sacrifice.

7. *Ecce Agnus Dei ("Behold the Lamb of God...")*

A few changes have been made to the translation of this prayer that comes shortly before holy communion is distributed, including the following:

"Happy are those who are called to his supper" is now "Blessed are those called to the supper of the Lamb"

In the previous translation of this prayer, the priest said the words, "Happy are those who are called to his supper" as he held up the Eucharistic host shortly before holy communion. But the new translation highlights even more how the Eucharist is no ordinary meal. The new words more directly recall a climactic moment in the book of Revelation when Jesus comes to unite himself to his people in a great heavenly wedding feast. In this scene, Jesus Christ, the Lamb of God, is depicted as a bridegroom intimately joining himself to his bride, the Church. An angel announces this loving union by saying, "Blessed are those who are invited to the marriage supper of the Lamb" (Revelation 19:9).

In the new translation, the priest at Mass more clearly echoes the angel's invitation to the heavenly wedding supper of the lamb. Here, we see how the Eucharist we are about to receive involves an intimate, loving communion with our Lord Jesus—one that is likened to the union shared between a husband and wife. Indeed, holy communion is a participation in that heavenly wedding supper of the Lamb, which celebrates the union of Jesus with his bride, the Church.

"Lord, I am not worthy to receive to you" is now "Lord, I am not worthy that you should enter under my roof"

These new words reflect the humility and trust of the Roman centurion in the gospels who asked Jesus to heal his servant who is at his house, paralyzed and in distress. As a Gentile, outside of God's covenant, and a Roman officer in charge of a hundred soldiers who were oppressing God's people, this centurion humbly acknowledges, "Lord, I am not worthy to have you come under my roof." Yet he expresses a great faith that surpasses that of many others in the gospels and amazes even Jesus: he believes Jesus can heal from afar, simply by speaking his word: "But only say the word, and my servant shall be healed" (see Matthew 8:8; Luke 7:6-7). Jesus praises this man for his faith.

Like the centurion, we, at this moment in the Mass, recognize our unworthiness to have Jesus come sacramentally under the "roof" of our souls in holy communion. Yet just as the centurion believed Jesus was able to heal his servant, so do we trust that Jesus can heal us as he becomes the most intimate guest of our souls in the Eucharist.

A Time for Spiritual Renewal

We are standing at a unique moment in the Church. As we have read, the new translation of the Mass represents the most significant liturgical development for English-speaking Catholics since Vatican II. For nearly forty years, Catholics have become quite familiar with the English translation of the Mass: "We believe in one God...Holy, holy, holy Lord, God of power and might...It is right to give him thanks and praise...." Many of us have heard these words since childhood and know them by heart, simply out of routine. So ingrained in us are these responses that if someone were to say, "The Lord be with you," many of us would instinctively respond, "And also with you."

But what do these words mean? Sunday after Sunday we recite these prayers and perform certain rituals. But what is the meaning of all we say and do in the liturgy?

The revised English translation provides a unique occasion for Catholics to reflect on the *meaning* of the Mass. As we have seen, many of those familiar words for the Mass parts will be changing. We will need to learn new responses and new musical settings. It is my hope that this period of preparation and transition will not be merely *mechanical*—simply about training people to say new responses—but *catechetical and spiritual.* As we are taken out of our routine, we have a unique opportunity to ponder anew what we say and do in the Mass and rediscover the splendor of the liturgy, so that we might grow deeper in our communion with Jesus every time we go to Mass.